First World War
and Army of Occupation
War Diary
France, Belgium and Germany

29 DIVISION
Divisional Troops
Divisional Cyclist Company
1 March 1916 - 30 April 1916

WO95/2291/1

The Naval & Military Press Ltd
www.nmarchive.com
Published in association with The National Archives

Published by

The Naval & Military Press Ltd

Unit 10 Ridgewood Industrial Park,

Uckfield, East Sussex,

TN22 5QE England

Tel: +44 (0) 1825 749494

www.naval-military-press.com

www.nmarchive.com

This diary has been reprinted in facsimile from the original. Any imperfections are inevitably reproduced and the quality may fall short of modern type and cartographic standards.

© Crown Copyright
Images reproduced by permission of The National Archives, London, England, 2015.

Contents

Document type	Place/Title	Date From	Date To
Heading	WO95/2291/1		
Heading	29th Division Divl Troops 29th Divl Cyclists Company Mar-Apr 1916		
Heading	29th Divisional Cyclists Arrived Marseilles 27.3.16 From Egypt 29th Divisional Cyclists March 1916		
Heading	Cyclist Coy Vol I Bef From MEF		
War Diary	Suez	01/03/1916	15/03/1916
War Diary	H T Lake Manitoba	16/03/1916	31/03/1916
Heading	29th Divisional Cyclist Company April 1916		
Heading	Cyclist Coy Vol II		
War Diary	Beauqusne	01/04/1916	03/04/1916
War Diary	Acheux	04/04/1916	30/04/1916

b995/2291/1

29TH DIVISION
DIVL TROOPS

29TH DIVL CYCLISTS Company.
MAR-APR 1916

29th Divisional Cyclists

Arrived MARSEILLES 27.3.16 from EGYPT

29th DIVISIONAL CYCLISTS

MARCH 1 9 1 6

29

Cyclist Coy
Vol I BEF
from M.E.F

WAR DIARY or INTELLIGENCE SUMMARY

Army Form C. 2118.

Cyclist Coy. 99th Div

Place	Date	Hour	Summary of Events and Information	Remarks and references to Appendices
Suez	1-16	6.40am	Physical Drawing 8.30 am. 65 N.C.O's MEN, Grenade School Remainder of Coy. Handling of Arms. Draft Rangers 2PM 4.30 pm For Lethbridge Handling of Arms	92.B
"	2 "	6.30am	do	93.B
"	3 "	6.30am	Physical Drawing Ariel Inspection 8.30am. Grenade School 65 N.C.Os Handling of Arms. Grenade School	93.B
"	4 "	6.30am	do Parade 8pm 8.30 am for Coy Route and Handling of Arms.	93.B
"	5 "	8.30am	do	93.B
"	6 "	6.30am	Physical Drawing 8.30 am. Route March. 5pm. Grenade School.	93.B 93.B
"	7 "	6.30am	Physical Drawing 8.30am. Sport Drill Coy. Remainder Grenade School 10am Draft Grenade School Remainder Signal Duty 11.30am Sanitation 5pm Grenade School	93.B 93.B
"	8 "	6.30am	Physical Drawing 8.30am Rifle Rd 10am to 12 noon. Rifle Exercise Grenade School 5pm Grenade School,	93.B 93.B
"	9 "	6.30am	Physical Drawing 8.30am. Coy Drill & Ceremonial 10.45am. Sport Drill and Coy Roof Grenade School 11.45am. Sanitation.	93.B
"	10 "	8.30am	Physical Drawing 8.30am Grenade School 10am to 12 noon Grenade School 5pm Grenade School 4.30 Pmt 6.30PM	93.B
"	11 "	6.30am	Divisional Operations	93.B
"	12 "	10am	Church Parades.	93.B
"	13 "	6.30am	Physical Drawing 8.30am. 11AM 12.30 pm. Grenade school.	93.B
"	14 "	6.30am	Physical Drawing 8.30am 11a 12.30 pm Grenade School.	93.B
"	15 "	6.30am	do	103.B
H.T. Lake Manitoba	16 "	11am	Embarked on H.T. LAKE MANITOBA at PORT SUEZ.	93.B
"	17 "	10am	Arms Inspection	93.B
"	18 "	10am	do	93.B
"	19 "	10am	do	93.B
"	20 "	10am	do	93.B
"	21 "	10am	do	93.B
"	22 "	10am	do	93.B
"	23 "	10am	do	93.B
"	24 "	10am	do	93.B
"	25 "	10am	do	93.B
"	26 "	10am	Arrived at MARSEILLES Disembarked for PONT REMY.	93.B
"	27 "	10am	On Journey.	93.B
"	28 "	10am	Arrived at PONT REMY. Left PONT REMY at 7pm arrived at LONG 10.5pm	93.B
"	29 "	6PM	Pioneer & Carpenter Instructor	93.B
"	30 "	10am	Left LONG. arrived at BEAUQUESNE 3pm.	93.B
"	31 "	8.30am		93.B

29th DIVISIONAL CYCLIST COMPANY

APRIL 1916

29

Cyclist Coy
―――――
Vol II

WAR DIARY
or
INTELLIGENCE SUMMARY.

(Erase heading not required.)

Army Form C. 2118.

Instructions regarding War Diaries and Intelligence Summaries are contained in F. S. Regs., Part II. and the Staff Manual respectively. Title pages will be prepared in manuscript.

Place	Date	Hour	Summary of Events and Information	Remarks and references to Appendices
BEAUQUSNE	1/4/16	10am	Arms & Equipment Inspection	94B
	2/4/16		Sunday	94B
	3/4/16	8:30am	Left BEAUQUSNE arrived at ACHUEX at 12 Noon	94B
ACHUEX	4/4/16		Controls of Roads and Observation Post	94B
	5/4/16		— do —	94B
	6/4/16		— do —	94B
	7/4/16		— do —	94B
	8/4/16	10am	Rifle & Bicycle Inspection	94B
	9/4/16	9am	Church Parade	94B
	10/4/16		Control of Roads and Observation Post	94B
	11/4/16		— do —	94B
	12/4/16		— do —	94B
	13/4/16		— do —	94B
	14/4/16		— do —	94B
	15/4/16		— do —	94B
	16/4/16	8am	Trench Digging until 4pm. Observation Post.	94B
	17/4/16		— do —	94B
	18/4/16		— do —	94B
	19/4/16		— do —	94B
	20/4/16		— do —	94B
	21/4/16		— do —	94B
	22/4/16		— do —	94B
	23/4/16		— do —	94B
	24/4/16		— do —	94B

Army Form C. 2118.

WAR DIARY
or
INTELLIGENCE SUMMARY.

(Erase heading not required.)

Instructions regarding War Diaries and Intelligence Summaries are contained in F. S. Regs., Part II. and the Staff Manual respectively. Title pages will be prepared in manuscript.

Place	Date	Hour	Summary of Events and Information	Remarks and references to Appendices
O CHEUX	25/7/16	8am	Trench Digging until 4 pm Observation Posts	9/3
	26/7/16		do — do —	9/3
	27/7/16		— do — do —	9/3
	28/7/16		— do — do —	9/3
	29/7/16		— do — do —	9/3
	30/7/16		— do — do —	9/3

www.ingramcontent.com/pod-product-compliance
Lightning Source LLC
Chambersburg PA
CBHW081254170426
43191CB00037B/2151